THANK YOU FOR YOUR PURCHASE!

QUICK TIP!

Add a blank sheet of paper

Amazon's paper works great with colored pencils. However, we recommend placing a blank sheet of paper or cardstock behind the page to prevent any bleed-through if using wet mediums like markers.

Congratulations! You've reached the end of the book.

We hope you enjoyed coloring these pages as much as we enjoyed designing them for you. If this book brought a smile to your face, we would be grateful if you could share your honest thoughts in a review by scanning the QR code below. If you don't know what to write, you can simply choose a star rating, which only takes a moment.

Your feedback means so much to us!

SCAN ME

Mia Birchwood

Made in the USA
Coppell, TX
13 November 2024

40146492R00046